30/30 HINDSIGHT

30 REFLECTIONS ON A 30-YEAR HEADACHE

TIMOTHY M. SHOREY

© 2019 by Timothy M. Shorey

Cover design by Daniel Lee

All Scripture references are from the *English Standard Version*, unless otherwise noted

ISBN: 978-1-64516-367-1

Dedicated to my Hon-Hon.

You have been what you promised:

My needed companion and friend

Contents

Prologue	**30/30 Hindsight** *(How This Came to Be)*	1
Reflection 1	**103° X 10D = N.D.P.H. X 365D X 30Y** *(How a Formula for Pain Gets Calculated)*	3
Reflection 2	**6.5 on the Richter Scale** *(How to Turn Pain into a Side-Bar)*	5
Reflection 3	**Five Days without Food** *(How I Starved for a Cure)*	7
Reflection 4	**The Pin Cushion** *(How We Went from Low to High and Back Again)*	9
Reflection 5	**Kindness Blindness** *(How It Hurts When Others Help)*	11
Reflection 6	**Affliction Pile-On** *(How to Process Hell on Earth)*	13
Reflection 7	**My Speed Governor** *(How the Father Enforces My Sabbath-Rest)*	17
Reflection 8	**The Only Dad My Kids Have Ever Known** *(How Pains Affects Personality)*	19
Reflection 9	**But What's a Ball For?** *(How Pain is Not an Excuse for Sin)*	21
Reflection 10	**The Most Important Thing about Me** *(How Beholding God Eases Headaches)*	23
Reflection 11	**The Rod of God** *(How God's Fatherly Heart Guides His Firm Hand)*	25
Reflection 12	**The Father Weeps** *(How Afflicting Us Grieves God)*	27
Reflection 13	**Someone with Skin On** *(How We Long for Someone We Can Relate To)*	29
Reflection 14	**He Took on Flesh** *(How God Became One of Us)*	31
Reflection 15	**A Frozen Tuna** *(How We Long for Someone Who Can Relate to Us)*	33

Reflection 16	**The Crown of Thorns** *(How Jesus Had an Accursed Headache)*	35
Reflection 17	**A Thorn in the Flesh** *(How a Bad Headache Keeps from a Big Head)*	37
Reflection 18	**I Pleaded Three (Hundred) Times** *(How Due Diligence Can Morph into Health Idolatry)*	39
Reflection 19	**In Weakness, Strength** *(How God's Sufficiency in My Pain Is My Best Sermon Ever)*	41
Reflection 20	**My Badge of Weakness** *(How I Love to Brag)*	43
Reflection 21	**24 Hour Increments** *(How Day by Day Grace Is the Only Way)*	45
Reflection 22	**Holy Taunting** *(How Bold Trash Talk May Be a Godly Thing)*	47
Reflection 23	**I'm Sorry, What Was Your Name?** *(How My Pain Affects My Memory)*	49
Reflection 24	**Blamers and Shamers** *(How Sufferers Have to Deal with Fault-Finders)*	51
Reflection 25	**Yes, I Do (Still) Believe in Gifts of Healings** *(How I Engage the Now, Not Yet, and Not-At-All Fight for Faith)*	53
Reflection 26	**In Sickness and in Health** *(How Marriage and Faith Are Covenantal Leaps)*	57
Reflection 27	**Promises Made and Promises Kept** *(How My Bride Has been All That, and More)*	59
Reflection 28	**My Headache, Her Heartache** *(How My Beloved Lives Inside My Skin)*	63
Reflection 29	**Light Momentary Afflictions** *(How Present Trials Produce Eternal Glories)*	65
Reflection 30	**No More Tears** *(How Pain Makes You Long for Heaven)*	67
Epilogue	**Can I Hear a Well-Done?** *(How I Live to Hear Him Say It)*	69

Prologue

30/30 Hindsight
(How This Came to Be)

"Blessed be...the Father of mercies and God of all comfort,
who comforts us in all our affliction,
so that we may be able to comfort those who are in any affliction,
with the comfort with which we ourselves are comforted by God."
(2 Corinthians 1:3, 4)

December 11, 2018

Here's something I bet many of you wish you could say: I've only had one headache in the past 30 years. No lie. Just one headache in all those years!

The trouble is that as of January 11, 2019, I have had that one headache *for* all those years. Every day, all-day with neither stop nor break nor relief. Lots of my friends know about this so it isn't a news-flash. But as I have crossed a milestone that few others ever achieve—a 30-year-long incessant headache—it seems like a good time to reflect.

Please don't misunderstand my heart: my trial isn't any worse than what many others have to face. In fact, I know very well and with great sadness, that others are far more deeply afflicted than I. Please know, too, that I do not want to compare pain by measuring mine up against yours. Each person's story is too real and too raw for that.

What makes my affliction different for me is that it is mine. It isn't yours or somebody else's. It is mine—and so it is part of the story that God has written for me, and part of the story that I think He wants me to share with others.

Which is what I've set out to do. Strange as it may seem, I have taken 30 days (plus two for this Prologue and an Epilogue) to mark my very personal, rather dubious achievement; to share 30 reflections that I've written about my 30-year crazy chronic cranial crisis. Call it 30/30 hindsight. If you have any interest in reading about the highs and lows and joys and sorrows of my experience, feel free to check these out at your leisure.

I wouldn't expect anything especially profound, if I were you. This is more a simple set of not-always-connected observations and insights; each of them exactly 500 words long (thanks to a creative and prolific use of contractions and hyphens!). I've written these to be an enduring record of grace for any who might be curious, in hope that those interested might get something out of them. But then again, *you* may not. If not, then perhaps you could pause to praise and pray. Praise because the Father's grace has brought me safe thus far. And pray that His grace will lead me all the way Home.

By the way, there are many more profound and comfort-rich books on suffering than this small work could ever hope to be. My goal is not to match them or replace them, but to accompany them; possibly to be a whispering echo to their thundering truth. Perhaps as I reminisce and reflect, my own experience of grief and grace will touch people in simple ways. Maybe in reading how another pilgrim through this hurting world has made it this far, you might be encouraged to keep on going, yourself. May God's comforts to me become your comforts, too.

In His grip,

Tim

1

103° X 10D = N.D.P.H. X 365D X 30Y

(How a Formula for Pain Gets Calculated)

*"The pain that gnaws me takes no rest...
[I]t is good for a man that he bear the yoke in his youth..."*
(Job 30:17; Lamentations 3:27)

December 12, 2018

My headache really isn't the crazy chronic *cranial* crisis that I previously claimed. More precisely it is a nasty never-ending *nerve* nuisance and nemesis.

Almost thirty years ago, when the nemesis first struck, I was a 30-year-old guy minding my own business. As pastor of 100 and father of five, I had plenty of business to mind. Yet He who knows such things better than I clearly felt that I didn't have enough. So on the day He appointed—January 11, 1989—I contracted a virus (probably viral meningitis), which pounded me with permanent nerve-damaging viral-force trauma.

The equation goes like this: 103° X 10D = N.D.P.H. X 365D X 30Y. I had a 103° fever for ten straight days which left me with what headache specialists term N.D.P.H. This has continued 365 days a year for the past nearly 30 years. N.D.P.H. stands for **N**ew **D**aily **P**ersistent **H**eadache. The **N**ew part of that highlights that it did not exist before then. One day no headache; next day boom. What wasn't before, now *was*. And is.

Daily defines the headache as an every-day condition. I wake up with it, do everything I do through it, go to bed with it, and would (if not for some

Advil-PM that helps me sleep) stay awake—or be woken up—because of it. The **P**ersistent part of my affliction doesn't just mean that it keeps going; it means that it keeps going no matter what pain-killers or treatments we use to counter-attack it. Like the time we tried a double or triple dose of Codeine along with muscle relaxants for three days. Believe me: while most of my body was feeling nothing at all, my head was still hurting. That is the definition of *persistent!* By January 11 it'll be 10,957 persistent days in a row (that includes seven leap years).

There you have it: $103° \times 10D$ (Days) = N.D.P.H. $\times 365D$ (Days) $\times 30Y$ (Years). Not surprisingly, it's a sure formula for pain and sorrow. But believe it or not, it is an even surer formula for grace and joy! That'll be my story in coming reflections. But for now, as the 30-year milestone approaches, I'll let Lamentations 3:19-32 be my testimony:

> "...[T]his I call to mind, and therefore I have hope:
> The steadfast love of the Lord never ceases;
> his mercies never come to an end;
> they are new every morning; great is your faithfulness.
> 'The Lord is my portion,' says my soul, 'therefore I will hope in him.'
> The Lord is good to those who wait for him, to the soul who seeks him.
> It is good that one should wait quietly for the salvation of the Lord.
> It is good for a man that he bear the yoke in his youth...
> For the Lord will not cast off forever...
> he will have compassion according to
> the abundance of his steadfast love..."

Truth.

2

6.5 on the Richter Scale
(How to Turn Pain into a Side-Bar)

*"[We are]...as sorrowful, yet always rejoicing; as poor,
yet making many rich;
as having nothing, yet possessing everything."*
(2 Corinthians 6:10)

December 13, 2018

I've been asked two questions more times than I can count. The first is "How bad is it?"—the assumption being that my headache can't be *that* bad since I'm still standing in a semi-sane state. So it's no surprise that people jaw-drop when I answer that on a Richter scale the pain is always at least a seismic 6.5. Without a whisper of exaggeration, whenever I pause to think about my pain, an actual deep sharp penetrating head-filling ache is always there, lurking for my attention.

Head colds compound the pain, moving the needle toward 8 or 9. On a bright shiny day, I always need sun-glasses. The pulsating noise of wedding receptions creates pulsating pain. When I'm in a big crowd in a small space, it will throb. Saddest of all, it *really* hurts to sing. If I sing praise with as much holy and happy gusto as I want—I cannot make it through even one song without mind-numbing pain. So I live at 6.5, and fluctuate upwards and back from there.

"So how do you function?!?!" (with that much punctuation) is the almost automatic second question. And I answer with equally automatic and emphatic impulse: *by the grace of God!*

For example: God has given me much grace to compartmentalize my pain; to set it over to the side so I can focus on what's in front of me. Maybe that's hard to imagine, but survival depends on it. I tell my pain where it belongs, move it over there, and then proceed with life. Essentially, that makes my pain a sidebar, and keeps it from becoming my focus, identity, or primary life narrative. Its place is in the margins, not the main text. It is not the story; it only accompanies the story.

The story is about Jesus and truth and devotion and family and church and mission and laughter and food and drink and song and love and mercy and justice—all bathed in the beauty and radiance of God. Not enough that I simply side-bar my pain, I have to center life with a positive focus; an energy for God and others. Tellingly, I feel my pain the most when I'm not doing anything, when I'm not channeling my energy into enjoying and doing good. It hurts the most when I do the least.

There's a lesson in there somewhere. Without becoming simplistic, can I suggest that we *not* let our narrative be defined by our griefs or grievances. Instead, let's offer ourselves to relieve others' pain, as a means of triumphing over our own. Jesus said it is more blessed to give than to receive. There's surpassing joy in self-giving living; joy sufficient to distract us from the intensity of our afflictions, and to fill our life with contentment in Christ, and in His creation and people. Sorrowful, yet always rejoicing. Poor, yet making rich. Having nothing, yet possessing everything.

3

Five Days without Food
(How I Starved for a Cure)

*"O taste and see that the Lord is good.
Blessed is the man who takes refuge in him."*
(Psalm 34:8)

December 14, 2018

On a lighter note, I love food. Not to be confused with a foodie, I am much more, a glutton. Supposedly, foodies have "a refined interest in food, and don't eat out of hunger but as a hobby." That makes me laugh. There's nothing refined about my interest in food. We gluttonous-types are simply hungry, and love to eat. I love the sensation, the taste, the feel, and when available, the sheer volume. Mark it down: food is never better than when there's lots of it.

My appetite doesn't really curb. With a bottomless and side-less pit, meals feed but seldom fill—making Spirit-enabled self-control a holy war. A sage once said: "What most people need isn't more push-ups, but more push *aways*." By and large, that wisdom—empowered by the Spirit—helps me rein in my indulgence. Of course it means that I leave nearly every meal still truly hungry. But if I didn't, I'd weigh 483 pounds by now.

Food reminds me of an early diagnostic effort for my headache. When a doctor wanted to test for contributing food allergy factors, he offered me two options. First was the old trial and error method which would've cut certain foods out systematically to see if pain would disappear when a food group did. But I wasn't buying into that nonsense, since I knew that a slow hit-and-miss process would drive me nuts. The alternative was simply to go without food for a week. Pretty straightforward: if food-related there would be a change in my headache with the removal of food. I chose to go with five foodless days rather than endless weeks of trial and error. Besides, my doctor told me that the hunger would diminish after a couple of days.

Reassured by his promise, I decided to turn this into a semi-monastic retreat of sorts. I collected my Bible, a few books, and a trunk load of water, and went away to a sparse college campus dorm room; as far away from Gayline's delicious culinary delights as possible. You know: Flee temptation and all that sort of thing.

Be it known that my doctor lied. Starting the week typically hungry, I finished it wildly ravenous. My whole body craved. *Everything* growled its hungry displeasure. And my headache, which started the week at 6.5, finished it at 9.5. Hence: one of the most physically miserable weeks of my life. Five days of total head-pain and hunger!

I'm looking for a lesson. Maybe it's: beware of doctors who say it won't hurt. Maybe it's about self-control, or delayed gratification for a greater good. Or maybe it's simply that there are times when the only thing you can do is cry in the moment, then later on have a good laugh at your own expense, and then finally, simply marvel at the grace that got you through! Yeah, let's make that my takeaway. Starving for a cure, I tasted God's goodness.

4

The Pin Cushion
(How We Went from Low to High and Back Again)

"[N]either shall there be mourning, nor crying, nor pain anymore"
(Revelation 21:4)

December 15, 2018

About 20 years after my food debacle, I was in a world-class headache hospital doing due diligence in pursuit of new options; the latest being a nerve block. It was a little unnerving (pun, perhaps unforgivably, intended) when the doctor stuck a needle into my head, full of a Novocain equivalent. Then he repeated it—not once or twice or ten times, but as many as thirty times—creating a pronounced pin cushion effect. Adding to the surreal was the crunch Gayline heard from across the room every time the needle pierced through whatever exists between skin and skull; a sound not unlike a pencil-point piercing Styrofoam (cue the wise cracks).

But the result was overwhelming. As the Novocain effect took hold, my whole head went numb. For the first time in 22 years I was pain free. There. Was. No. Pain. I was stunned by the sensation; a release I cannot describe; a soaring exhilaration unlike anything I've ever felt before or since.

As Gayline and I wept for joy, I asked how long it would last. "Between 30 minutes and the rest of your life. Everybody's different," the doctor said. That turned tears into rivers. For the first time in 22 years I was pain free, and even better: I had hope that it would last. O the joy!

Before I finish my story, let me say this: probably the best way I can help you know how much my head hurts, is to say that I would gladly receive that same 30-injection treatment every month if it'd give me that relief in between. Absolutely.

The problem is that there was no relief in between. Within 30 minutes the pain began to return. By the time we left the hospital it was back to my norm. And by the time we got home, it was a 9.5. Then we wept again, as floodgates of lost hope opened up. We went from our highest happiest point to our lowest—in less than an hour.

I don't share this for your pity. God has given me so much grace that I need no pity. Still, this might help you sense what chronic sufferers feel. High highs and low lows. Hopes raised and hopes dashed. Crazy remedies and crushing disappointments.

But what I most want you to see is what I saw: a glimpse of heaven. Revelation 21:4 reads differently now—*"He will wipe away every tear from their eyes, and death shall be no more, neither shall there be mourning, nor crying, nor pain anymore, for the former things have passed away."*

I now know what *vanishing pain* feels like. I've had a foretaste of Freedom Day, when an eternal pain release will happen in all who believe. My pin-cushion experience, however fleeting, has helped me look forward to Then; when in a twinkling instant, all that makes us weep, will be no more.

Come, Jesus, come!

5

Kindness Blindness
(How It Hurts When Others Help)

*"Weep with those who weep...
Bear one another's burdens and so fulfill the law of Christ."*
(Romans 12:15; Galatians 6:2)

December 16, 2018

I've woken up early this morning. Headache caused, I'm sure, since eyes opened to a 7.5 ache. Gayline will come downstairs in a bit. Having noticed my early rise, she'll probably ask about my pain. I'll give her that look she's seen a thousand times, and she'll feel the pain of my pain one more time. She will express her heart simply in a returning look of love, knowing well how that is all there is to do. Just care.

Without speaking for all chronic sufferers, I'd suggest there are times when the best and only thing to do *is* care. Not to make kind people regret good-intentions, but some are so kind that when pain is mentioned, they go looking hard for a solution (usually it's been kindness, though sometimes it's been opportunism: a chance to push a favorite dietary or product agenda). Friend, it may be hard to see, but when a chronic sufferer is asked, "Have you tried this?" or even worse, is *told*, "I know what can help you", the help can hurt—especially when there's expectation that the sufferer will act on the recommendation.

I call this *kindness blindness*. When well-meaning folks press chronic sufferers to try their approach, they seem blind to the obvious. For unless too poor or proud to try, every normal long-term chronic sufferer will have tried *many* potential remedies, and likely will know where to find others. So there's little need to suggest another.

Don't get me wrong: I'm nourished by people's kindness—and it will receive Heaven's reward. But I've lost count of how many healing professionals I've seen—and all the traditional and alternative remedies I've tried. I've been evaluated by two world class headache centers, three other neurologists, five different chiropractors, one osteopath, multiple allergist/nutritionist-types, two acupuncturists, various therapists, assorted general practitioners, and more.

I've tried no caffeine and some caffeine, strange nutrition drinks and bee jelly, fewer work hours and lots of sleep, nerve blocks and deer antler pills, TMJ exercises and physical therapy, even painful pins and needles—and of course: Advil, Aleve, Excedrin, Tylenol, Percocet, two or three other prescription pain meds (with names long forgotten), and Codeine.

What people like me most need is *not* another thing to try. In kindness, please don't think you need to find a fix; just find some time to pray. Let your hurting friends know you're thinking of them. Signal them somehow that you haven't forgotten. Offer them an appropriate reminder of your care, and assurance of ongoing prayer. Follow that with heavenward praise for a grace so great that it can awaken suffering folks (like me) with hope, even after 30 years of pain. All these will do some precious good!

By the way, when Gayline came down this morning she did give me exactly the same heartfelt look that she's given me so often before; which was enough.

My pain didn't need to be fixed; just felt.

6

Affliction Pile-On
(How to Process Hell on Earth)

*"For you cast me into the deep, into the heart of the seas,
and the flood surrounded me;
all your waves and your billows passed over me."*
(Jonah 2:3)

December 17, 2018

When things seem as bad as possible, they actually aren't. My dad often quipped: "Things ain't never so bad but what they could be worse"; and he was right. And sometimes life seems determined to prove it, producing its "affliction pile-ons" (though my headache seems neither to notice nor care).

When head-pain sees other stuff piling on, it doesn't take a day off. Instead, it's an ever-present pain filter through which everything happens; including a perfect storm of trials that happened from December 24, 2004 through December 1, 2006:

- Christmas Eve, 2004: a child gets cancer
- January, 2005: my dad and mom's already advanced cancers worsen
- February, 2005: a dear ministry partner steps aside
- March, 2005: unspeakable tragedy hits a church family
- April 2005: our child almost dies
- May, 2005: I have excruciating tooth pain requiring

- emergency dental work (while keeping vigil over our child)
- June, 2000: some people we love dearly, need crisis care
- July, 2005: another child is hospitalized
- August, 2005: our church building program requires my massive labor attention
- September, 2005: we visit very ill parents
- Christmas Day, 2005: my dad dies
- January, 2006: my mom's condition worsens
- January, 2006: a child is hospitalized again
- March, 2006: Gayline's dad (with four prior heart attacks) has heart surgery
- May, 2006: a sister gets cancer
- June-August, 2006: ongoing care of the sick
- November, 2006: I spend five weeks in bed with bulging disks
- December 1, 2006: my mom dies

All that with a 6.5 (or worse) headache. It's just the way it was.

Actually, it was worse. But you'd not believe it if I told you. Many would believe it, though, since it sounds painfully familiar. Change the dates and details, but keep the waves and billows, and it's a storm-page torn from their (your?) personal journal.

Lots of people would describe their experience of affliction pile-on as "hell on earth", but not me. My heart won't let me. To love Jesus rightly, I need to know—and I do—that all these trials (even if intensified by 1000°) are not *near* hell on earth. They may be hell-*ish* (bearing a faint likeness to sufferings in hell—like a pin-prick is "spear-ish"), but they are not *hell*; a distinction that I need to preserve lest I distort reality beyond recognition.

The gospel teaches that Jesus is the only One who has ever truly experienced hell on earth. He bore it—the fullness of God's just and holy wrath over sin—in His body and soul, during the darkened hours of Calvary. And because He got infinitely worse than He deserved, we will get infinitely better than we deserve. Jesus deserved nothing but Heaven, and we, nothing but hell. Instead He bore our hell and we receive His Heaven.

When my afflictions seem somewhat hellish, I need to remember this humbly. Because He actually endured hell here on earth, I'll never experience it—either here, or there.

Sing Hallelujah! What a Savior!

7

My Speed Governor
(How the Father Enforces My Sabbath-Rest)

"The Sabbath was made for man, not man for the Sabbath."
"Come away by yourselves to a desolate place and rest a while."
(Mark 2:27; 6:31)

December 18, 2018

If you've ever driven a go-cart, you'll know that the buggy will only go so fast. It's frustrating for Jimmy Johnson wannabes, but:

> With the pedal
> To the metal,
> At that speed
> You'll have to settle.

The reason is that the engine is rigged with a speed governor; a device regulating how much fuel gets in, in order to limit acceleration. There's nothing you can do about it. It's not going to go any faster no matter how hard you press it to the floor.

    I've been given a speed governor. My constant 30-year-long headache pain regulates (and depletes) energy flow in my body, keeping me from exceeding a healthy speed in life. When I race and chase without rest, I crash and burn. Excessive ministry labor for even 36-48 hours comes with a pain and exhaustion price tag that I simply cannot afford. Actually a merciful gift, pain does for me what I believe I would not have been able to do for myself. I sincerely doubt that I would've been willing or able to maintain proper speed, without God rigging my engine.

You see, contrary to how people joke, faithful pastors don't work just one day a week. They have to exert an almost superhuman will to *keep* from working seven days a week. I work six days a week, averaging around 55 hours of ministry per week. But even with that, I still end each week with a list of ministry and people needs easily as long as the list I just completed. My temptation is not laziness, but the idolatry of busyness and self-importance; the vanity of trying to be omnipresent and omni-competent for everybody.

Pastors often kill their souls and damage their families by over-work. Preachers' kids grow up to hate the church because their dads were there for the church *more* than for their families. Children, wives, and spiritual health all become collateral damage.

I thank God for my speed governor since it's forced me to get home to rest. I've had no choice but to keep a carefully guarded schedule that includes rest and replenishment time; something that I'm convinced has preserved me from burn-out, and from being an absentee husband and dad.

Truth is, our Creator has given us all a speed governor. It's called Sabbath rest. When God rested on the seventh day, it wasn't because He was tired and needed a break. It was because He knew we'd get tired and would need a break. He established restful pacing and Sabbath spacing to limit our frantic racing and endless chasing: one day a week to go slower and gaze higher.

It's a life rhythm worth keeping. In my case, for the good of body, soul, and family, the Lord installed a back-up plan. He gave me an ever-present pain-activated speed governor because I was all too likely to disconnect the Sabbath one.

Practice rest; lest He give you one as well.

8

The Only Dad My Kids Have Ever Known
(How Pain Affects Personality)

"Oh, that I were as in the months of old, as in the days when God watched over me, when his lamp shone upon my head, and by his light I walked through darkness, as I was in my prime..."
(Job 29:2-4a)

December 19, 2018

Everything I have experienced in the past 30 years has been pain-baptized. Every breath I have breathed; every baby I have diapered; every child I have bounced on my knee or wrestled on the floor; every tear I have wiped (or wept); every correction I have given and family moment I have nurtured; every festive holiday I have enjoyed or grieving season I have endured; every ball I have bounced or racket I have swung or log I have chopped or mile I have walked; every sermon I have preached; every grieving, sinning, hurting, yelling, accusing, struggling, back-sliding, and stumbling church member I have pursued, loved, comforted, corrected, and restored; every funeral I have led; every wedding I have cheered; every book I have read; every prayer I have prayed; every marital embrace I have felt; every temptation or trial I have faced; every argument I have had; every angry impulse I have processed; every laugh I have released; every sorrow, joy, victory, defeat, or pie slice I have tasted—every single one of all these has been experienced through non-stop unrelenting pain.

That *does* something to you. Pain affects personality. Chronic pain alters people; making a lasting difference in who they become, and are.

I am different than I was 31 years ago, as Gayline would sorrowfully agree. Personality dimmed when headache dawned. I don't last long at parties and weddings (Gayline's missed lots of wedding cake because of me). Excitement stays muted. No long vigorous hikes. Creative fun saps my energy even to conceive, never mind, do. Roller coasters were out decades ago. Pain makes me sit still; exactly how you spell *boring*. It wasn't always this way, but it is now—and nobody's been affected more than Gayline.

And the thing is: this difference is pretty much all that my children and grand-children have ever known. Since headache onset happened when they were very young or still unborn, my different is their same.

They don't know how loud I used to laugh, how many endless hours I could play basketball, how I loved the noise and nonsense of huge family gatherings, how late I could stay up, how vigorously I could belt out ten straight songs, how freely I would kid around, how recklessly I would throw myself into football.

They've always and only known that Daddy and Grand-daddy's place is where loud voices and rambunctious rollicking need to be checked at the door. Grand-daddy needs naps, avoids raucous games, and finds his chair as quickly as possible. They wouldn't know that the pre-headache me was a really cool guy! Well, not actually ever cool; just more enthusiastically and energetically present.

But this hope I have: a new me is coming, and it'll make the old me look so *yesterday*. Tomorrow's me will sing, dance, run, laugh, feast, and praise—making my kids and grand-kids fill up with wide-eyed amazement as they watch Grand-daddy go!

9

But What's a Ball For?
(How Pain is Not an Excuse for Sin)

"...God is faithful, and he will not let you be tempted beyond your ability..."
(1 Corinthians 10:13)

December 20, 2018

One long-ago evening, as I collapsed into my easy chair to recover from another pain-filled day, our four-year-old walked out of the toy closet with a 16-inch rubber ball. Seeing this triggered an instantaneous, rather sharp, through-my-pain reaction against impending ball bedlam: "David don't throw that around. And don't be bouncing it either." The dear child paused with befuddled look, eventually finding appropriate words to respond to my abrupt commands: "*But Dad, what's a ball for?*"

I realized my unreasonable demands too late. My alarm over the impending noise and motion hurricane was an understandable pain-affected defensive instinct. Weary with pain, all my nerve endings were on high alert. Every impulse was to preempt additional ball-induced pain. So without careful thought (or thoughtful care), I let my pain speak.

In that last paragraph I first wrote that my response was a "*pain-produced*" defensive instinct, but then settled on pain-*affected*. *Produced* is too strong; something I've had to keep in mind over these 30 years. While pain may affect (or tempt to) sinful reactions, it doesn't produce them; my heart does (Mark 7:14-23; James 4:1-3). The difference is pretty massive— and I have had to be ruthless with my conscience in the light of it.

Early on I sensed the spiritual vulnerability connected to my hurt. It's too easy to indulge sin, and then blame it on the pain. So I'm very grateful that from the start the Holy Spirit etched 1 Corinthians 10:13 into my frontal lobe (etched so deeply, I can almost feel it)—"*No temptation has overtaken you that is not common to man. God is faithful, and he will not let you be tempted beyond your ability, but with the temptation he will also provide the way of escape, that you may be able to endure it.*"

In the 1 Corinthians 10 context "temptation" includes testings that tempt; hard circumstances that produce sin enticements. And by means of a promise Paul declares emphatically that circumstances never excuse sin. God promises that no matter what my test, there is always a way out—always grace enough to resist the temptation; and conversely, never an excuse to give in to it.

This promise means there are no free passes. Pain may make sins understandable, but never excusable. I cannot rant or overeat or drink to excess or vegetate too long or go to forbidden places on the Internet, and then pull out *pain* as my own personal get-out-of-jail-free card. Pain never justifies sin. It simply defines the circumstantial context in which God calls me to holiness, *so that* His sufficient sanctifying grace can be magnified in my life.

I take this promise as also, my shield. Just as I do not *get* to sin because of my pain, I also do not *have* to sin. The Father's overcoming grace will be ever-and-always enough, even when the ball ricochets wildly onto a collision course with my head.

10

The Most Important Thing about Me
(How Beholding God Eases Headaches)

*"He heals the brokenhearted and binds up their wounds.
He determines the number of the stars;
he gives to all of them their names."*
(Psalm 147:3, 4)

December 21, 2018

A.W. Tozer once said, "*What comes into our minds when we think about God is the most important thing about us.*" If so, then Isaiah 40 is a well from which we often must draw. God heralds comfort there (40:1, 2) to His exile-afflicted people (39:5-7) by offering a simple invitation: "*Behold your God*" (40:9)—and then pulls back the veil that we might do just that. That invitation still stands.

Gaze at God.

Nothing so restores the ruined, so strengthens the weak, so comforts the sorrowful, so lifts the fallen, so sustains the infirmed, so raises the downcast, so binds up the broken, so heals the wounded, so satisfies the hungry, so dignifies the downtrodden, and, yes, so comforts the headache, as does a frequent, persistent, life-long gaze of the soul upon the being and beauty of God. If you want grace for all of life, make an adoring vision of God the daily impassioned pursuit of your life.

When we allow who God is to meet us where we are, there is sweet comfort. This is the essence of grace, and it is the theme of the Shorey story. Thirty-five years ago, as a 25-year-old pre-headache pastor, I preached through Isaiah 40, summarizing it like this: "*There is one true God who owns a place of supreme dominion over all people, destinies, nations, and creation, by which he irresistibly governs the universe, personally sustains all things, and freely and perfectly accomplishes his will; to the end that glory might crown his name and good might come to his people.*"

More recently, I've preached and summarized it like this: *God over all, because of Christ, gives strength to the trusting weary in his time according to their need, to do the remarkable for his glory.* Everything in that summary is either explicitly or implicitly in Isaiah 40—forging an anchor for the tempests of life.

One great comfort is the phrase "God over all". "*It is he who sits above the circle of the earth...*" (22). God sits enthroned *above*, as sovereign King and ruling Shepherd (10, 11). From there He rules:

1. Over every nation (15-17, 22-24)
2. Over every limitation (like ignorance [12-14], or space [22], or weakness [10, 26], or fatigue [28])
3. Over every imitation (18-20)
4. Over all cross-examination (27)
5. Over all creation (12, 25, 26, 28)

God creates, numbers, and sustains the galaxies (26). By one estimate, the observable universe contains 100,000,000,000 galaxies and 1,000,000,000,000,000,000,000,000 stars (that's one septillion, with 24 zeroes). That's only an educated guess, but our sovereign God needn't guess. He knows them all—and has a name for each.

This is so comforting. By knowing this God, we don't need to know anything else. We can live with a headache, and without answers (knowing He has them all)—which means that the most important thing about us is realizing that it really isn't about us, after all.

11

The Rod of God
(How God's Fatherly Heart Guides His Firm Hand)

"Suffering produces endurance, and endurance produces character, and character produces hope."
(Romans 5:3, 4)

December 22, 2018

Why is God afflicting me? Think with me about human nature, and you may find an answer.

Have you ever wondered why kids are wired so crazily? Promise a child praise and prizes for not touching a hot stove, and he will be all the more determined to touch it. But if he sneaks a touch, he will never touch it again. There's a lesson there.

Pain teaches better than praise. Offer a toddler rewards for good behavior, and he will not conform for long. Make consequences for bad behavior unpleasant enough and he will learn it doesn't pay. No doubt, such behavior modification through consequences doesn't produce a good heart. But it does help to curb bad behavior—which is better than nothing! I should know: I was once a kid, *and* I've had six of my own.

But it's not just kids. Sentimentalists (who I imagine must never watch the news or raise toddlers or look in the mirror) often gush about innate human goodness. But I believe that Adam's fall into sin so corrupted our spiritual DNA that usually, whatever our age, we need suffering to learn goodness. Leave us to follow natural instinct without painful consequence, and it'll get ugly fast.

This helps me handle my headache. I have made peace with my headache because God has remade *me* through my headache. Unwaveringly committed to help me grow up in faith and love, the Father appointed a 30-year headache for me. And it has done me great good.

"*'My son, do not regard lightly the discipline of the Lord, nor be weary when reproved by him. For the Lord disciplines the one he loves, and chastises every son whom he receives'...God is treating you as sons...[and] he disciplines us for our good, that we may share his holiness. For the moment all discipline seems painful rather than pleasant, but later it yields the peaceful fruit of righteousness to those who have been trained by it*" (Hebrews 12:5-11).

"*Suffering produces endurance, and endurance produces character, and character produces hope*" (Romans 5:3, 4). Likewise, "*the testing of our faith produces steadfastness*" which, in its "*full effect*", makes us "*perfect and complete, lacking nothing*" (James 1:2-4). No wonder we should consider it "*good*" when we are afflicted (Psalm 119:67, 71), and "*count it all joy when we meet trials of different sorts*" (James 1:2-4).

I have no doubt that my headache has made me a better and humbler man, a more dependent, caring, and disciplined person, a more need-aware, grace-amazed, and praise-awakened child of God; yes, *far* more than I would otherwise have been. So *I kiss the rod of God*, for by it I have learned grace, character, and hope. Suffering sanctifies.

People in denial don't feel their pain like I do; so if you're wondering about that, don't. I'm not denying my pain; I'm simply saying that it's worth it. Where pain is, gain happens.

12

The Father Weeps
(How Afflicting Us Grieves God)

*"And after you have suffered a little while, the God of all grace,
who has called you to his eternal glory in Christ,
will himself restore, confirm, strengthen, and establish you."*
(1 Peter 5:10)

December 23, 2018

I can kiss the rod of God because I know that He applies it with a breaking heart. Lamentations 3:33 says that *"He does not afflict from the heart"* (or as one puts it, *"He does not enjoy hurting people"*). *Afflicting* is not something He takes any pleasure in. Rather, it is something that has to happen because it's the best way for my sin-stunted faith to grow.

God is not a sadist. When He sees me ease my aching head into a pillow with ever-so-careful effort to find some relief, He isn't fiendishly uncaring, smirking over my pain. Instead, He feels it with me. I know this because of Jesus, who once said that when we see Him we see the Father (John 14:9). So when we read of Jesus weeping over human suffering while on earth, we see the heart of God. The Father is known and His grace-filled love is seen in the life and laments of Jesus (John 1:14-18).

God the Father's discipline is like my dad's. Dad would sometimes say, "This really is going to hurt me more than you. I don't *want* to do this." I've said that, too; to my kids. Children aren't buying it of course, but that doesn't mean that it isn't real. It really does hurt us more than it hurts our kids when we have to do or permit the things that make them weep. Still, we discipline because we know that without it they will never reach their life potential. To withhold discipline—as anyone paying attention in this permissive age will know—is to keep children from achieving their very best. Still, to apply discipline is a sorrow beyond words.

I believe that the Father's heartache over my headache is deeper than mine. He cries when I cry. And yet, the Father, in His infinite wisdom and boundless love, ordains my sorrow to His sorrow, so that when the nighttime is over, morning joy can come.

And morning joy will come. Nighttime is never forever. The night of weeping will pass, and a sunrise of laughing joy will dawn—with the length of the first, and the timing for the second being decided by the One who will make it all beautiful in His time (Ecclesiastes 3:1, 4, 11). *"The LORD will not cast off forever...though he causes grief, he will have compassion according to the abundance of his steadfast love..."* (Lamentations 3:32). With fatherly compassion, *"...He knows our frame; He remembers that we are dust"* (Psalm 103:13, 14).

Because our Father disciplines with love, our pain literally will end *as soon as possible*. When His purpose for our pain is complete, the pain will be no more; not lasting one millisecond longer than necessary. Count on it: a loving Father would do no less.

"Father, I do count on this, but would you please hasten the dawn? Nighttime is hard."

"I hear you my son; Christmas is coming."

13

Someone with Skin On
(How We Long for Someone We Can Relate To)

"That which was from the beginning [God's Son], which we have heard, which we have seen with our eyes, which we looked upon and have touched with our hands, concerning the word of life—the life was made manifest..."
(1 John 1:1-2a)

December 24, 2018

Pain was my 4:00am alarm today. So random! Usually unannounced and always unwelcome, it snatches sleep away—leaving me tired from the get-go. Good news is that I've got a day off, so I can take a nap whenever I want! I'm going to need it.

Contrast me to rambunctious four-year-olds. Perpetual motion, they bounce around with seemingly boundless energy; jumping, skipping, racing, climbing—all without ever coming to a complete stop. I cannot relate.

Except: they don't actually have boundless energy. They just spend their energy with reckless abandon, as whirling tornados of wild chaos—until the plug gets yanked. That's when they crash into deep sleep with stunning suddenness. And that's when I realize that I can relate to them after all. None of us is cordless.

But God is. He never gets weary (Isaiah 40:28). He never naps or needs a good night's sleep. He doesn't have to be plugged in. Must be nice. What must it be like, being God? Who is this God that never needs to rest, re-charge, or rejuvenate? What kind of Being has an infinite self-existent power of being (and doing) in Himself? He is so different from me, so transcendent, so very *other*. I live tired. He is never tired. Hard to relate to.

Years ago, I read about a child who, frightened by a nighttime storm, called out, "Daddy, I'm scared!" When his daddy called back (from under his snug covers), "Don't worry, son. God loves you and will take care of you", a few seconds of silence ensued. Then came the plaintive reply: "I know God loves me, but right now, I need somebody with skin on."

It's hard relating to Someone, however great or good, who has no skin. But the unrivalled truth of our faith is that we don't have to. Christians remember the birth of Jesus tomorrow—the incarnation of God the Son. Christmas celebrates when God put some skin on; thereby becoming Someone we can far more easily relate to. John tells us how he heard the incarnate Son of God, seeing Him with his eyes, and *touching* Him with his hands (1 John 1:1, 2). God's Son has real, touchable skin!

When God wrapped Himself in skin, He had to scratch mosquito bites. He got splinters in Joseph's woodshop. He skinned His knees, scraped his elbows, bruised his shins. He had distinct fingerprints. In real skin and flesh and blood, Jesus got tired and fell fast asleep. He got thirsty and hungry. He sweated, bled, felt searing pain, and died. In fact, the skin on His now risen hands and feet is everlastingly nail-scarred.

By sharing skin-wrapped existence with us, God became then, and is now, a Person we can relate to easily. Such sweet comfort for life and for eternity!

For soon and very soon we are going to *touch* the King.

When He and I meet, we will hug.

14

He Took on Flesh
(How God Became One of Us)

*"[T]he Word became flesh and dwelt among us,
and we have seen his glory...full of grace and truth...
No one has ever seen God; the only God,
who is at the Father's side, he has made him known."*
(John 1:14, 16-18)

December 25, 2018

Merry Christmas to one and all!

Christmas proves that God is not a cruel sadist who delights in our pain or a helpless observer who cannot heal our pain, but a willing sharer who enters our pain and a mighty deliverer from our pain.

In the crown jewel of Christmas texts, Paul writes of Jesus, eternal Son of God and God the Son: "...*[He who] was in the form of God, did not count equality with God a thing to be grasped, but emptied himself, by taking the form of a servant, being born in the likeness of men. And being found in human form, he humbled himself by becoming obedient to the point of death, even death on a cross*" (Philippians 2:5-8).

Notice the strangely connected phrases, "...He *emptied* himself, by *taking*...". How do you empty by taking? Don't you empty by taking *out* or taking *away*? Yet, Jesus, who was in the form of God (the exact shining forth of God's being), made Himself less by taking on more. Someone has called this *subtraction by addition*. By adding a human nature to His divine, He emptied Himself.

If I have a brand new shiny-bright $200,000 Lamborghini in all its "glory", and then add a bumper sticker, I have subtracted by adding. When it comes to perfection, more is less. You don't improve a filet mignon by adding ketchup.

The pre-Bethlehem Son of God was God the Son, resplendent in the majesty He enjoyed with the Father and Spirit forever, in the presence of adoring angels. So, by agreeing to "add on" a human body and nature (Hebrews 10:5-7), He subtracted; not to the diminishment of His actual deity but to the temporary diminishment of His visible blazing glory.

The Word (God, the Son) who was in the beginning, and who was with God, and was God (John 1:1) became flesh. By this condescending love He now dwells among us (John 1:14). In this He became Emmanuel; God with us and one of us (Matthew 1:23). By partaking of our flesh and blood, He unashamedly made us true "brothers" in the human experience (Hebrews 2:11-14).

Here is a God like no other. He is neither distant nor disinterested. He doesn't stand by idly while we suffer. Even less does He inflict suffering with sadistic glee. Heaven forbid. Instead, He has entered our world of pain, to share in the pain, to deliver from the pain.

God, the Eternal Son laid aside His majesty to enter my shame. He removed a crown of glory to wear a crown of thorns. He took on all the headaches of being human so He could rescue me from all my headaches (physical and spiritual) once and for all! I need nothing more.

> *"Veiled in flesh the Godhead see*
> *Hail the incarnate deity!*
> *Pleased as man with men to dwell*
> *Jesus, our Emmanuel."*
> (Charles Wesley)

O come, o come, let us forever adore Him.

15

A Frozen Tuna
(How We Long for Someone Who Relates to Us)

*"For we do not have a high priest who is unable
to sympathize with our weaknesses,
but one who in every respect has been tempted as we are..."*
(Hebrews 4:15)

December 26, 2018

One of my headache specialists had all the empathy skills of a frozen tuna. Mouth slightly agape. Eyes glazed. Cold as ice. Really, this guy was the worst. Back when I told him that I had had a headache for decades, had been to a dozen-plus doctors, and had been tested, scanned, MRI-ed, blood-worked, medicated, dieted, exercised, vitamined, nutritioned, therapized, acupunctured, and adjusted, all he could do was scold me because I hadn't tried hard enough.

I think he could've used a good stiff two-week headache to thaw him out a bit; to make him more than a headache specialist. As a headache sufferer he might have become a headache sympathizer, which would actually have made him a better headache specialist. Truth?

At least he would've been better able to relate.

When Christmas happened, Emmanuel arrived to live in our world with us. What that means is that *God-with-Us* is more than a specialist; He's a sympathizer. He hasn't just diagnosed and prescribed. Rather, He has come to relate to us, to feel what we feel.

"*Since therefore the children share in flesh and blood, he himself likewise partook of the same things...[H]e had to be made like his brothers in every respect, so that he might become a merciful and faithful high priest in the service of God...For because he himself has suffered when tempted, he is able to help those who are being tempted...For we do not have a high priest who is unable to sympathize with our weaknesses, but one who in every respect has been tempted as we are, yet without sin. Let us then with confidence draw near to the throne of grace, that we may receive mercy and find grace to help in time of need*" (Hebrews 2:14-18; 4:15, 16).

You see, we can go boldly to the throne of grace because Jesus' came willingly into our valley of grief. He knows what we need because He once needed it Himself.

The old spiritual originally lamented, "*Nobody knows the trouble I've seen; Nobody knows my sorrows.*" Happily, along the way someone noticed the bad theology and changed the last two words: "*Nobody knows, but Jesus.*" Jesus knows all the trouble I've seen. He knows it because He knows it (like He knows everything), and He knows it because He has experienced it. Which is what it means that His name is Emmanuel. He is with us that much.

We've all been hungry, thirsty, tempted, beaten down, afraid. So has the Man of Sorrows. We've all tasted betrayal, having loved people dearly, only to have them turn on us. Jesus has been there. We've all been misunderstood. People actually mistook Jesus for a *demon*. We've all had people fail us in times of need. Remember Gethsemane (Matthew 26:37-40). We've all wondered where the Father was. On the cross, the Savior wondered the same (Matthew 27:46).

Somebody knows the troubles I've seen. Glory! Hallelujah!

16

The Crown of Thorns
(How Jesus Had an Accursed Headache)

*"...Christ redeemed us from the curse of the law
by becoming a curse for us..."*
(Galatians 3:13)

December 27, 2018

Our treason is the reason for the season. Christmas happened so Good Friday could happen. And Good Friday had to happen because of our treason against God. He answered our rebellion with redemption.

Jesus' one recorded "headache" demonstrates this. It is safe (though superficial) to say that when He wore a crown of thorns (Matthew 27:29), Jesus, like me, had a headache. Only His pain seared, and His headache was different. Indeed, to call His thorn-crowned condition a "headache" minimizes the perverse and trivializes the profound.

His crown of thorns was perverse; a sick moment when twisted humanity looked God right in the eyes and decided to mock. Like sixth grade playground thugs, they thought it would be fun to bully their Maker.

But the crown He wore was even more profound than perverse. Consider that thorns were not a part of pristine creation, but only started to grow in Genesis 3, in fallen creation. They did not exist when everything was "very good" (Genesis 1:31), but only after everything was sin-cursed (Genesis 3:17, 18). Thorns exist, because sin does. Thorns are a punishment; an accursed consequence of human rebellion.

That explains what happened long after Bethlehem, at the trial of Jesus. When God allowed monstrous humans to press thorns into Jesus' head, it revealed something so profound, so affecting, so fearful, so wonderful, that it beggars words. By wearing thorns, Jesus was bearing the curse. Indeed, He was bearing the curse *away*. In that thorn-crowned moment, God was saying to us: "Behold My sin-bearer and curse-breaker. Now under My curse, He will surely carry all your sins in His body onto the cross, and break their curse forever." Jesus bled and Jesus died, to reverse the curse.

You may recall that Jesus "*[became] obedient to the point of death, even death on a cross*" (Philippians 2:8). "Even death on the cross" is *not* a way of saying "even the *agonizing* death of crucifixion". It's a way of saying "even the *accursed* death of crucifixion". As Scripture says: "*...Christ redeemed us from the curse of the law by becoming a curse for us—for it is written, 'Cursed is everyone who is hanged on a tree...'*" (Galatians 3:13).

Jesus wasn't just willing to die; He was willing to be cursed under the wrath of God. By submitting to the crown of thorns and hanging on a Tree, He submitted to the curse of God. In effect, God chose to curse Himself to bless us.

That He had a headache like me is a comfort. That He wore the thorns for me is eternal redeeming love.

God came down for Man to die
Mercy, justice reach the eye
Wrath unleashed upon Himself
Curse reversed, Incarnate stealth
Never once has man devised
Such just forgiveness; mercy, wise.

See! God reveals His glory here
He bows, He stoops, He comes, draws near
Wrath and love on Calvary kiss
True glory, wonder, mystery, this.

17

A Thorn in the Flesh
(How a Bad Headache Keeps from a Big Head)

> *"And we know that for those who love God*
> *all things work together for good,*
> *for those who are called according to his purpose.*
> (Romans 8:28)

December 28, 2018

Do you have your go-to parts of God's Word? I do. For comfort, there's Isaiah 40. For identity in Jesus, there's Ephesians 1-3. To see Christ's majesty, there's Hebrews 1. For a heavenly hug, there's Romans 8. For a reminder of who wins, there's Revelation 19-22.

And for *purpose in my pain*—the help needed during seemingly senseless affliction—there's 2 Corinthians 12:7-10. There Paul writes:

"*So to keep me from becoming conceited because of the surpassing greatness of the revelations, a thorn was given me in the flesh, a messenger of Satan to harass me, to keep me from becoming conceited. Three times I pleaded with the Lord about this, that it should leave me. But he said to me, 'My grace is sufficient for you, for my power is made perfect in weakness.' Therefore, I will boast all the more gladly of my weaknesses, so that the power of Christ may rest upon me...For when I am weak, then I am strong.*"

Paul had some incredible spiritual privileges (that's what "*surpassing greatness of revelations*" refers to); enough to make any normal man pretty full of himself. So an affliction "was given" to him to keep him from becoming conceited. What it was we do not know, though I'm partial to the view that it was headache related. Whatever it was, it was given to diminish Paul's pride of self-sufficient superiority. Chronic affliction: God's pride smack-down.

I'm no Paul, but I have been privileged. I've heard the gospel since birth. I had godly parents. I've had great teachers and have witnessed supernatural gifts—along with ministry opportunities that many only dream of. I've never had a bad pastor. I've been reading and digesting theology since youth—with theology books coming out my ears. Wonderful partners in ministry, a happy marriage, beloved children, spiritual insight, 35+ years of ministry experience, preaching and writing gifts: all this can tempt toward self-sufficient pride.

Which is why I have a headache. Seeing my danger God gave me a thorn; a piercing painful persistent problem to remind me every single day that I cannot do anything unless He enables it; a stabbing thorn that bleeds my pride with relentless effect.

Paul says his affliction was God-given, but Satan delivered. The mystery of the heavenly realms is on display here. We know the thorn was God-given since it was given to keep Paul from becoming conceited (not something Satan would be interested in). We know it was Satan-delivered, because, well, Paul says so. I don't understand this invisible dimension of things, but I do know (1) that no trial ever gets to me without God's consent, and (2) that whenever Evil gets involved God still wins (Genesis 50:20).

Satan wants my headache to create doubts about God's love. God wants it to create doubts about myself; leading to reduced head size and increased reliance on Him.

God will have His way.

18

I Pleaded Three (Hundred) Times
(How Due Diligence Can Morph into the Idolatry of Health)

*"[O]ur God whom we serve is able to deliver us
from the burning fiery furnace [or a fierce headache],
and he will deliver us out of your hand, O king.
But if not, be it known to you, O king,
that we will not serve your gods or worship the golden image."*
(Daniel 3:17, 18)

December 29, 2018

Do you remember my frozen tuna doctor who scolded me for not trying hard enough? There are heath-and-wealth gospel-types who scold Paul for the same. In 2 Corinthians 12:8 he tells us that he prayed three times that the Lord would remove his thorn. Why just three times? Maybe if he had prayed four times, or had named it and claimed it. Maybe if he had "word-faithed" it into happening. Maybe if he had exercised more "authority" in Jesus' Name to "command" the affliction away. Maybe he just didn't try hard enough.

Actually Scripture doesn't say he never asked again; it only says that after the third time God assured him of grace for his affliction. He might have prayed 100 more times. We just don't know. But it's also possible that three times were like three witnesses to Paul. In Scripture three witnesses were sufficient to confirm something (e.g.-2 Corinthians 13:1). Did Paul feel that the Lord, by three denials, had confirmed that He wasn't going to heal—at least for the moment?

Or, more likely, was the Lord's promised sufficient grace all the answer he needed? Could it be be that he treasured sustaining grace more than healing grace? It's possible that once assured of God's ongoing strength, he craved nothing more. There's a thought: *healing from affliction isn't everything; having God's grace in affliction is* (more on that at another time).

Some people have wondered if I've tried hard enough to find a headache cure—either through prayer or medicine or alternative treatment. Here's my response. I believe in due diligence—by pursuing prayer and medical or alternative remedies responsibly and in faith. But if I've prayed repeatedly (in my case 300+ times), if I've seen dozens of doctors, and if I've tried many options, then I've done my part, even though my long headache persists. Clearly, God's purposes for my pain continue, and so the pain will, too; at least for now.

I should want to be healed and try to be healed, but not obsess to be healed. There's an important difference between due diligence to find healing, and idolatrous desperation to be healthy. Too many people worship the golden image of Self; offering millions in free-will offerings to the deity called "Health", and pursuing endless dietary rites, exercise rituals, and wholeness ceremonies in an obsessive devotion to "well-being". That's not for me.

I promise you: I try to eat right, sleep right, exercise right, medicate right, and pray right. But I won't be chasing all over the globe for a remedy when Jesus has already given me all I need: grace for each and every day. I've got a family to love, a church to serve, a world to reach, a life to live. Somehow I don't think God wants me to waste it all in search of a cure.

I aim, instead, to worship the Healer, not health.

19

In Weakness, Strength
(How God's Sufficiency in My Pain Is My Best Sermon Ever)

"And I was with you in weakness...
and my speech and my message were
not in plausible words of wisdom,
but in demonstration of the Spirit and of power,
so that your faith might not rest in the wisdom of men
but in the power of God.
(1 Corinthians 2:3-5)

December 30, 2018

Consider these words again: "...'My [i.e.-Jesus'] *grace is sufficient for you, for my power is made perfect in weakness.' Therefore, I* [Paul] *will boast all the more gladly of my weaknesses, so that the power of Christ may rest upon me... For when I am weak, then I am strong*" (2 Corinthians 12:9, 10).

And now this: "...*[W]e have this treasure in jars of clay, to show that the surpassing power belongs to God...So we do not lose heart. Though our outer self is wasting away, our inner self is being renewed day by day*" (2 Corinthians 4:7, 16).

Paul says that what makes him strong is Christ's power *in*, or *by*, his weakness, and that it is as the treasure of the gospel is carried in fragile *jars of clay* that the surpassing power of God is clearly shown.

I know what that is about—not theoretically, but actually and truly. I calculate that over 36 years, I have preached 1,600+ sermons, counseled for nearly 15,000 hours, planted a couple of churches, and devoted more than 95,000 hours to the ministry of the Word and prayer. But my headache is the most fruitful part of my ministry.

While some express appreciation for sermons I've preached in the past; *more* express gratitude for my headache's effect on their faith. In fact, the one sermon that's received the most long-term appreciation is one in which God's grace through my headache features prominently. The real life illustration that my headache is—of God's truly sufficient strength—has touched many with lasting blessing.

It's pretty humbling. Not my eloquence. Not my style. Not my great wisdom or insight. None of these has preached the most effectively. Don't misunderstand: I'm not diminishing the need for truth proclaimed. I'm just saying that, in my experience, what has preached most compellingly is the truth *proclaimed* married to the truth *proven*. And the truth proven, has been proven through my pain.

People have let me know many times that when they had a headache "the other day", they thought of me. And when they thought of my headache they thought of the God who sustains His children over the long haul. And then they trusted God to face their own pain in life. How amazing is that?

When thirty years of pain don't reduce a man to a puddle, but somehow are met with daily renewed *inner man* strength, there is something more at work than an indomitable human spirit. It is the power of God; evidence that all the grace that God has promised is a grace that will be delivered. I've been renewed with joy day by day for 30 years. That is the hand of God alone; a hand that *you* can trust today.

This is all very humbling. The most powerful part of my ministry is me at my weakest. God's sufficiency in my pain: my very best sermon ever.

20

My Badge of Weakness
(How I Love to Brag)

"I will bless the Lord at all times;
his praise shall continually be in my mouth.
My soul makes its boast in the Lord;
let the humble hear and be glad."
(Psalm 34:1, 2)

December 31, 2018

"But he said to me, 'My grace is sufficient for you, for my power is made perfect in weakness.' Therefore, I will boast all the more gladly of my weaknesses, so that the power of Christ may rest upon me. For the sake of Christ, then, I am content with weaknesses...For when I am weak, then I am strong" (2 Corinthians 12:9, 10).

Paul says he is content with, and *boasts* in, his weaknesses. Contentment and pride while in affliction: most of us would see the first as remotely possible, but then consider the second utterly ridiculous. Wouldn't you say?

But not me. I'm with Paul. I will just say it: I wear my badge of weakness with humbled holy pride. I love to brag about it! I'm not just passively content with my headache, I actually boast in it. In fact, I'd boast in it daily to everybody, if not for the fact that some might think I'm talking about me. It'd be easy to assume that in talking about 30 years of endurance through pain, I'd be boasting in myself. But that would miss the point by a mile.

I wear my weakness badge because it gives me a chance to boast in God. I will brag again even now: I glory in my headache because it has been an astonishing source of joy in my life. I know without doubt that I have tasted the sweetness of all-sufficient grace more exquisitely because of my weakness than I ever would have if the ordeal had never happened. The experience of God's gracious strength through pain has been more precious than gold; so precious, in fact, that it is more dear to me than healing.

I've often imagined God coming to me and saying, "Tim, here are two options: (1) you can be healed of your headache right now, but with that healing you will *not* feel as much of my everyday grace-filled renewing strength as you have for these 30 years; or (2) you can keep the headache for the rest of your life, but with that I will keep pouring a daily conscious enjoyment of My amazing renewing grace into you. What's your choice?"

The decision would be absolute no-brainer easy. Without hesitation, I'd keep the headache. Even as I type through pain right now, I am here to say that sustaining grace is more precious than healing grace. Daily awareness of God's renewing presence through His Word and Spirit is simply an inexpressible joy.

So I wear my badge with pride. I will boast, both now and forever, in the sufficiency of grace and in the surpassing worth of Jesus' replenishing love, grace, truth and power.

Now, truth be told: if Jesus were to come to me and offer me complete healing *and* an everyday delight in His amazing grace, I'd take that deal for sure! But then again, there's a word for that. It's called *Heaven*.

21

24-Hour Increments
(How Day by Day Grace Is the Only Way)

"Blessed be the Lord, who daily bears us up;
God is our salvation."
(Psalm 68:19)

January 1, 2019

I have long been committed to a 24-hours-at-a-time way of life. I sang it to Gayline at our wedding: *"Day by day and with each passing moment, Strength we'll find to meet our trials here..."* Then, at 23, when I was called into pastoral ministry and the terrifying prospect of 50 years of ministry lay before me, the Spirit reminded: "Tim, you aren't called to pastor for 50 years; you're called to pastor for today. Do today, and I'll do the rest." Nearly 37 years of 365 todays later, He hasn't failed me once!

Though this is survival for every part of my life, consider my headache. If I thought about doing 24 more *years* of pain, I'd say, "Put me out of my misery now". But if I think about doing 24 more *hours*, I say "Bring it on!"— not because I think I can, I think I can; but because I know He can.

Paul rings this day-by-day note in 2 Corinthians 4:16—"... *our inner self is being renewed day by day.*" It echoes in Isaiah's plea, *"O Lord, be our arm every morning, our salvation in the time of trouble"* (Isaiah 33:2). Then there's Jeremiah's affirmation: *"the steadfast love of the LORD never ceases; his mercies... are new every morning..."* (Lamentations 3:22, 23). We overhear it in the psalmist's bed-time prayer, *"Satisfy us in the morning with your steadfast love, that we may rejoice and be glad all our days."* (Psalm

90:14). For those who missed it, David turns it into it praise: *"Blessed be the Lord, who daily bears us up; God is our salvation."* (Psalm 68:19). Even Jesus keeps it *daily* in his model prayer, *"Give us this day our daily bread."* (Matthew 6:11); then commanding it in His famous sermon, *"Therefore do not be anxious about tomorrow, for tomorrow will be anxious for itself. Sufficient for the day is its own trouble."* (Matthew 6:34).

Here's some unsolicited advice this New Year's Day. I suggest that you start this new year by thinking in terms of one day: *to*-day. Make a New Year's resolution to live this *day*, not this year; to do January 1 well, more than 2019 well. Life is best lived—and trials are best faced—when we live in 24-hour increments, and leave our yesterdays and tomorrows to God.

This is an essential life-secret. Without it we languish in yesterday's regrets or tomorrow's concerns. We waste our lives fretting over what's past and done, or overwhelmed by what may or may not yet be. By dragging the past into today or letting the future invade our *now*, we burden our hearts either with what we cannot ever change, or may not have to face.

We are not meant to do life this way. Thankfully, I am blessed with an everyday headache that reminds me that in fact, I *cannot* do it this way.

My conclusion?

Have a Happy New.................Day!

22

Holy Taunting
(How Bold Trash Talk May Be a Godly Thing)

"If God is for us, who can be against us?"
"Death is swallowed up in victory.
O death where is your victory?
O death where is your sting?"
(Romans 8:31; 1 Corinthians 15:54, 55)

January 2, 2019

I once had a recurring nightmare in which demonic monsters chased me through dark and dangerous perils. In the premier, not knowing that it was a dream, or what would happen, or how it would end, I was terrified throughout. But I escaped the danger, and awoke, alive and well.

Things were different in the rerun; reason being that though the monsters and dark dangers were exactly the same, I wasn't. I was different because early on I recognized the monsters from my previous adventure, and realized while still in the nightmare that it was only a nightmare. So these night terrors could do me no harm. This turned my terror into taunting. Instead of screaming in fear, I openly mocked the things that had once made me afraid.

It's amazing the difference, when we know the outcome. Knowing that God over all is for us—that He rules and over-rules everything, turning it for our good—we can face life with all its traumas and terrors, sporting what's been called, a 'holy smirk'; that subtly sarcastic confident look of those who know how the nightmare ends.

There's a place for godly taunting, bold spiritual trash-talk, and a "holy smirk". Two biblical examples come to mind. The first is when Elijah taunts the false god, Baal. In the famous Mount Carmel showdown (1 Kings 18), Elijah challenges Baal (and his minions) to go head-to-head with God. But when Baal fails to show up, Elijah scorns God's enemies, taunting them to pray a little louder to get their god's attention. After all, Baal might be sleeping or musing or on a trip or taking a bathroom break (yes, all that is in the text; 18:26-29). The point is not that we are to mock people who have been deceived into believing lies, but that we need not fear anyone who pretends to be God or anything that threatens to do us harm. After all, *"He who sits in the heavens laughs, and holds them in derision"* (Psalm 2:1-4).

Paul does his own holy apostolic trash-talking in 1 Corinthians 15. Having proclaimed Christ's resurrection and the certainty of ours to follow—a resurrection to life eternal and immortal (15:1-54)—he taunts death with the Easter words that have echoed down through the centuries: "Death is swallowed up in victory. O death where is your victory? O death where is your sting?" That is some serious trash-talk there! "Death: you're nothing. We win! End of story!".

Friends: these 30 reflections on my headache are me trash talking. In Christ, I mock my pain even as I weep it. "Pain: you've got nothing. Satan: get behind me. Get outta my face! Suffering: I scorn your vain efforts to ruin me. You are weak. Jesus and I win!

> O headache, where is your sting.
> O pain, where is your victory?
> Thanks be to God who gives me the victory
> through Jesus Christ my Lord."

23

I'm Sorry, What Was Your Name?
(How My Pain Affects My Memory)

"We are afflicted in every way, but not crushed; perplexed, but not driven to despair."
(2 Corinthians 4:8)

January 3, 2019

Besides how my headache mutes my singing (keeping me from singing as loud and long as I'd like), I think I grieve most over how it affects my memory, in connection to my relationships.

Once upon a time I had vice-like recall. I could remember names and specific conversations a year after the fact with detailed precision: who said what; and when and why and where. Now I often cannot recall what I said or to whom—a *day* after the fact. And then there's my problem with names. I grieve daily because I cannot remember names without extreme effort combined with repeated ongoing interactions.

Part of my memory issue is old age. Part of it is sheer numbers (I pastor a pretty active church with lots of people coming and going—which makes for a constantly fluctuating list of names to remember). Part of it is because in a growing church, conversations with each individual are infrequent.

But a big part of it is my headache. Conversations take everything I've got. As a brother and pastor, my conversations involve leaning in to listen, observing body language, processing people's emotions, empathizing, assessing needed care, praying in the conversational moment (for pastoral wisdom and prophetic insight), thinking (to recall relevant biblical truth), pausing (to ponder how to answer), choosing what to say (or if the situation calls for it, to say nothing at all), and then actually *saying* something, if it's needed. Then, if the conversation extends beyond a few seconds, all of those mental and spiritual-emotional efforts have to be sustained over time, and then repeated numerous times in any given day and week. And all this happens through 6.5+ degree pain.

The end result? I burn so much energy in a conversation that I have little or none left after the conversation to actually file it (or names) away in my memory. Remembering takes mental work which takes strength, and that, by the time a conversation is over, is in short supply.

So when my memory fail happens again, and I have to ask "I'm sorry, what is your name again?" or "Can you please remind me of what we talked about?"—please know my grief. Loss of a sharp memory has been an acute sorrow, especially when it offends or wounds people I love.

Parting comment: did you notice how in the last reading I taunted pain, but in this one I grieved it? Chronic sufferers are like that. In an eye's blink, we can move from taunting confidence in Christ to tearful weeping in trial. Or we can feel both simultaneously. That's me. Right now I could taunt my pain or mourn it. It depends on which side of me I choose to express.

Behold my complexity and perplexity. I live here—joyful, but afflicted and confused. And if, in the process, I seem to have forgotten your name, please remind me with grace.

24

Blamers and Shamers
(How Sufferers Have to Deal with Fault-Finders)

*"His disciples asked, 'Who sinned, this man or his parents,
that he was born blind?'
Jesus answered, 'It was not that this man sinned, or his parents,
but that the works of God might be displayed in him.'"*
(John 9:2, 3)

January 4, 2019

Are you familiar with Job's friends? They were blamers and shamers, assaulting that woebegone man with accusation and insinuation. Cruel comforters, they (Job 4-25). Skilled fault-finders, they didn't realize that usually God allows His children to suffer, not because they've done something bad, but because He intends to do something good.

I haven't had many blamers and shamers. I've mentioned Dr. Frozen Tuna who faulted my effort. Other doctors patronized, like I was a child imagining it all. Occasional name-it-claim-it types questioned my faith because prayers for headache-healing didn't work. Some self-appointed remedy-hunters copped an attitude when my "Thank yous" for their suggestions didn't bubble effusively enough. Then of course, was my own heart which searched me carefully; hunting for sin behind my suffering.

That last one is worth reflection. Truth be told, while Scripture indicates that most suffering is *not* caused directly by a person's sin (e.g.-see Job 1-2 and John 9:1, 2), Paul indicates that occasionally it is. For example, he warns that if we share in the Lord's Supper unworthily—with unconfessed sin, unresolved conflict, and unexamined heart—we can eat and drink God's discipline on ourselves. For this reason, *"many...are weak and ill, and some have died"* (1 Corinthians 11:17-32). Sometimes the Lord does afflict His people because of sin in their lives; something humble sufferers will take to heart.

Minimally, Paul's words compel an honest heart check. Do I have a secret life? Any hidden sins, yet unconfessed? Any habits in the dark that need to be brought into the light? How is my marital fidelity? Sexual purity? Financial integrity? Parental and pastoral responsibility? Internet and entertainment accountability? Basic honesty? Devotional discipline and delight? These are great spiritual diagnostics, and whatever provokes them is truly a blessing. So I praise God again for my pain, since it has moved me to search my heart.

But be forewarned: sufferers all too often get stuck in introspection; mired in blame and shame. While honest self-reflection is good, a groveling, guilt-mongering "I-must-be-the-very-worst-of-sinners" self-flagellation isn't. While finding sin to confess is a spiritual triumph, finding reason to fear and self-loath isn't.

If my spiritual search engine finds no connection between my suffering and sin, then I need to move on. If I find a possible connection, then I need to confess my sin, remember that my hope is built on what is best: on Jesus' blood and righteousness; and then also move on, with assurance.

And if I have blamers and shamers assailing me, I should let them be. Their own turn at suffering without reason or relief will come. They will know better than they know now, in God's good time.

As for me, here is how I answer blame and shame, whatever its source: *"Who is to condemn? Christ Jesus is the one who died—more than that, who was raised—who is at the right hand of God, who indeed is interceding for us"* (Romans 8:34).

25

Yes! I Do (Still) Believe in Gifts of Healings
(How I Engage the Now, Not Yet, and Not-At-All Fight for Faith)

> *"To [one] is given faith by the same Spirit.*
> *To another gifts of healing by the one Spirit…"*
> (1 Corinthians 12:9)

January 5, 2019

I spoke to some collegians recently, mentioning my headache in passing. Predictably, a student asked afterward if she could pray over me for my healing. I was happy to let her do so, even though bold believing prayers have been prayed over me countless times—all seemingly to no avail. Still, I never ever refuse—because *Yes!* I do (still) believe in gifts of healings!

Here's my humble view when people want to pray for my healing:

1. 1 Corinthians 12:7-11 teaches that the Holy Spirit gives *gifts of healings* (in the plural) whenever He decides the time is right.
2. This means there aren't permanent *healers* per se, just healings; not any automatic name it/claim it healer-commanded miracles, but just sincere humble pleas for a here-and-now, *please-this-time* healing that the Lord may or may not give, depending upon His will and my spiritual needs.

3. Since I know that my Father loves me and doesn't enjoy hurting me (remember Lamentations 3:33), I know He will not afflict me even one second longer than is needed for my good.
4. Therefore, I am confident He will heal me as soon as His good purposes for my pain are complete.
5. And given that those purposes may have been completed a second ago, this person offering to pray over me right now just may be the means by which my healing will happen.

There. Now you know why I will keep on saying *yes* whenever people ask to pray for me; because this time may be *the* time.

The faith-fight we all have to engage is over the *now*, the *not yet*, and the *not-at-all*. While sometimes God's healing is *now*, and sometimes it is *not yet* (maybe not until Heaven), we must know it is never *not-at-all*. Healing will happen, for it really is guaranteed through Jesus' atonement (Matthew 8:16, 17; Isaiah 53:5). It's just a matter of time before we experience it.

I rarely doubt God's healing promises. What I most assuredly doubt is my sense of timing. What He intends as not yet, I think needs to be now. And when the now doesn't happen, I have to fight to not interpret not yet, as not-at-all; trusting that my time will come.

And until it does, I will keep believing that holding grace is as amazing as healing grace. For what really is the more astonishing miracle of God: a man being healed by grace in an instant, or a man being held by grace for 30 years? Eternity will sing them both.

As for me, I am content to live in the uncertain place between the temporary now and the eternal then. For it is in not knowing *when*, that anticipation, surprise and joy meet; creating a subtle faith-adventure in the uncertain anticipation of each new day. For who knows? This could be the day!

26

In Sickness and in Health
(How Marriage and Faith Are Covenantal Leaps)

*"[L]ove is as strong as death...the very flame of the Lord.
Many waters cannot quench love; neither can floods drown it."*
(Song of Solomon 8:6, 7)

January 6, 2019

Gayline and I celebrate our 41st anniversary tomorrow. So I'm thinking about marriage covenants (and headaches), today. Typically, marriage vows promise *"...to have and to hold you from this day forward; for better, for worse, for richer, for poorer, in sickness and in health, to love and to cherish, till death do us part..."*

It's a covenant that expects the unexpected. Anticipating that life will mess with us, often in unforeseen and unpleasant ways, we promise to remain true, come what may. Good times, and bad. Better circumstances, and worse. Richer seasons, and poorer. In sickness, and in health. Marriage involves these covenantal leaps. We jump in, never knowing where we will land.

Vows solemnize and sacralize our commitment to *stay*; whatever the vicissitudes of life (*vicissitudes*: fluctuating happy/unhappy situations; life's *ups and downs*), even though we cannot know what those ups and downs might include. It's a big ask, and a very big promise, indeed.

When Gayline pledged me her "in sickness and in health" love, she knew I'd get sick sometimes. What she didn't know was that she'd be marrying a 30-year-long headache (cue further wise cracks). That's a vicissitude she never envisioned, but throughout which—much to my joyous wonder—her love has remained unquenchably true (more on that in coming reflections).

I wonder how many Christians realize that faith is also a covenantal leap. Sincere faith in Jesus is a Marriage, indeed *the* Marriage, of which all other unions are but a shadow. In our confession, we covenant to make the Triune God *our* God, and to be one of His people. In baptism (a kind of spiritual wedding ceremony) we enter the water in the Name of the Father, Son, and Holy Spirit. By taking on God's Trinitarian Name, we declare that, come what may, we are His and He is ours.

As in marriage, we don't know all that this will involve. We don't know fully the sacrifices our Savior-Husband will ask of us, or the sufferings we will need to endure. Yet, because we so need and love Him, we willingly take faith's covenantal leap.

And why do we love Him so? Because God in Christ loved us first, wooing and winning our covenanted devotion with His prior covenanted love:

"Behold…I will make them dwell in safety…[T]hey shall be my people, and I will be their God. I will give them one heart…that they may fear me forever, for their own good…I will make with them an everlasting covenant, that I will not turn away from doing good to them…I will put the fear of me in their hearts, that they may not turn from me. I will rejoice in doing them good…with all my heart and all my soul" (Jeremiah 32:37-41).

Behold God's unfailing covenantal devotion: in sickness and in health, in headache and in heartache, come hellishness or high-water, we are forever His, and He, is forever ours.

27

Promises Made and Promises Kept
(How My Bride Has Been All That, and More)

*"This is my beloved and this is my friend...
I am my beloved's and my beloved is mine."*
(Song of Solomon 5:16; 6:3)

January 7, 2019

I remember Gayline's first Tim-targeted smile. I was undone. Dazed. Smitten. Captured. Hers. Losing man points here; but without a care. I'll sing the virtues of my bride until death do us part, and then will talk to Jesus about her for as long as He let's me keep talking.

I started calling Gayline *Hon-Hon*, short for Honey-Honey, nearly as soon as love ignited; making her my *double-hon* right from the start. Twice the sweetness—so to speak. Mysteriously, she loved me back; and with an astonishing love! Forty-one years ago today, these were her promises to me:

- *"I Gayline, believing that God has ordained our marriage, will strive by the grace of God to be your crown of virtue.*
- *"I pray that in everything I do, it will be for your good and not evil all the days of your life.*
- *"I, knowing that we are to bear, believe, hope, and endure in all things, together as one, desire to be to you your needed companion and friend.*

- "As the church is to love and obey its head, the Lord Jesus, in like manner I desire to love and obey you, my head.
- "I will lovingly give of my strength, the work of my hands, and the thought of my mind for the glory of God in your happiness."

My head fills. For these promises made, have been promises kept. My bride has been all that, and more: a woman of wisdom, faith, and devotion; committed to playing Lady Eve to my Lord Adam; ever and always alongside, to share the journey and serve the King.

Only she's had to be this to a man in perpetual pain; bearing me up when infirmity has so often taken me down. We were married at 19/20, and started sharing my headache at 30/31. Eleven years of marriage without pain; thirty years with. She got gypped. Yet she's wholeheartedly kept all her promises even though the man I am, is not *exactly* the man she married.

Here's an anniversary ode, in praise of my beloved:

My marriage bond is what I see
A wonder wrought in clay
A fine and rare simplicity
The Potter's chosen way.

There at my side with beauty graced
My wife, devoted friend
Whose aid in every duty faced
Brings task to joyful end.

Dear Father, gracious Potter-God
I bow in grateful stance
For you have made of earth and sod
The wife with whom I dance.

Please stand by me beloved wife
In simple elegance
And cast upon my earthen life
Your modest radiance.

Until this fragile pottery
Is worn and broken, old
Please be the match to favor me
'Till clay is turned to gold.

Then shall these vessels be returned
To where the Potter is
The mystery of marriage learned
Our love then lost in His.

My needed companion and friend—whose devoted love has been stronger than a thousand deaths.

28

My Headache, Her Heartache
(How My Beloved Lives Inside My Skin)

"The two shall become one flesh [body]."
"In [a] body...if one suffers, all suffer together..."
(Ephesians 5:31; 1 Corinthians 12:22, 26)

January 8, 2019

What happens to someone who lives with someone who lives with pain? I can't speak for all, but in our case, Gayline knows, and has lived with my headache for so long that it is hers as much as mine.

She reads the degree of my pain by the tilt of my head.

She discerns a 7.5 from a 6.5 by looking into my eyes.

She detects even my slightest pain-affected mood change with seeming sixth-sense awareness.

From across a crowded room she sees a posture droop or creased forehead that signals that it's time to act, lest I cross a pain threshold that will ruin me. Soon she appears at my side, and with a squeeze of my elbow suggests that it's time to go. Only then do I realize how much I hurt, and how tired I am.

She knows how a sequence of events will affect my head, long before I've given it any thought. She stands guard at my calendar gate to keep pain-orcs at bay. She instinctively slides the cushion behind my head as I get into the driver's seat—knowing that neck strain will jack up my head pain without it. She looks for bigger, softer chairs for me because she knows it matters. Without fail she will inform restaurant servers that we need a booth, because if I don't cushion my body, my head will seek revenge. To ensure needed rest and comfort she will check my pillow quality, book extra leg room on the flight, make sure where we're staying has a big enough bed, and discreetly set *end*-of-our-hospitality-and-fellowship times for our guests. She even *wants* me to watch the sports show in order to relax.

Truth be told: Gayline knows when I am *really* hurting before I do, and only later do I realize how much her sensitivity has rescued me again. She is noise monitor, calendar guard, crowd controller, comfort manager, pain-carer, and pain-sharer—all wrapped into one beautiful, faithful, and *hurting* person.

Yes, she hurts in all of this, too. She isn't only aware of my pain. She feels it. It's not just that she, like me, has skin on. It's that she's wearing *my* skin. Since in marriage math, *1+1=1*, she's me and I'm her; making my headache her heartache, felt for me every single day.

And not just *for* me. She feels it for herself—though she rarely, if ever says so. Yet how could my headache *not* affect her life, her dreams, her bucket list, her time, her social life; thereby creating her own set of losses and crosses beyond those she feels for me.

All this is to say: the next time you pray for me or for any chronic sufferer, please plead the grace of God for the people chronically suffering with the chronic sufferer; because what happens to someone who lives with someone who lives with pain is really hard to bear.

29

Light Momentary Afflictions
(How Present Trials Produce Eternal Glories)

> *"...Forgetting what lies behind and
> straining forward to what lies ahead,
> I press on toward the goal for the prize
> of the upward call of God in Christ Jesus."*
> (Philippians 3:13, 14)

January 9, 2019

In 1995, 199 Olympians were asked: "Would you take a drug to guarantee a gold medal even if you knew it would kill you within five years?" Reportedly, 100 said *Yes*. This radical commitment to a transient glory is something which few of us can relate to. It's tough to follow the logic that leads someone to pay the ultimate price for a passing prize.

But would you and I be willing to pay a passing price for the ultimate prize?

Meet the man, Paul. In 2 Corinthians we see that he's had a rough go of it. He has done time in a fully-stoked furnace. His recent past has involved prison time, several brutal muggings, hunger, exhausting work, sleeplessness, slander, and a whole ton of thankless effort. This poor guy needs a hug.

But don't tell him that. Notice how he responds to all of this (the half of which hasn't been told) with astonishing hope:

"*So we do not lose heart...For this light momentary affliction is preparing for us an eternal weight of glory beyond all comparison, as we look not to the things that are seen but to the things that are unseen. For the things that are seen are transient, but the things that are unseen are eternal"* (2 Corinthians 4:16-18).

Here are some hope-inspiring truths that ready us for suffering:

The present involves affliction; the future involves glory. Paul acknowledges affliction in the now (see also Romans 8:18, 19). He's not in denial; nor should I be. A thirty-year long headache is *not* nothing. But the future? That involves glory. Splendor. Honor. Praise. Immortality; infinitely *more* than nothing!

The affliction is light; the glory has weight. A thirty-year long headache is a weightless wafting wisp of smoke; lighter than air—compared to the awaiting glory. This glory has weight to it. Substance. Realness. It is to affliction what a ton of gold is to a fluffy feathery fleck of down.

The affliction prepares so that glory will surpass. A thirty-year long headache is *getting ready* a glory beyond all comparison. It doesn't produce defeat; it promises honor. It It doesn't punish, it prepares. It doesn't subtract; it adds. It isn't loss; it's gain.

The affliction is momentary and transient; the glory is eternal. A thirty-year headache—and longer if God so chooses—is a fleeting moment, the briefest of blips on the eternal screen, a passing shadow. But the glory that awaits—beautified and magnified through my pain—will simply never ever end.

All of this matters for my own personal Olympic event. For if I finish my headache marathon without complaint, and endure it with patient contentment in Christ, boasting in my weakness so that His strength can be revealed through me, I will get future, substantial, never-diminishing glory; the weight and honor of which only increase with every passing grace-sustained minute that I run!

A passing price for the ultimate prize.

Sign me up.

30

No More Tears
(How Pain Makes You Long for Heaven)

*"For to me to live is Christ, and to die is gain...
to depart and be with Christ is far better..."*
(Philippians 1:21, 23)

January 10, 2019

Today completes three uninterrupted decades of pain. Well, *almost* uninterrupted. There were those painless few minutes that 30 nerve-block injections produced.

I want painless again. Except this time, I want it to last. That, of course, can only happen if Jesus heals me *from* Heaven or heals me *in* Heaven. A taste of Heaven on earth, or the fullness of Heaven in Heaven. Any sane person would prefer the latter, but I'll take either.

Pain brings Heaven to mind, which is good. After all, God comforts us now with a promise of an eternal pain-free life (Revelation 21:3, 4). But I want to be careful. There's a wrong and right way to look upward. Wrong is the gloomy doomy way; a "hope" rooted more in weariness of earth than anticipation of Heaven. This is depression masquerading as hope; despair looking for escape; unbelief in God's present loving care expressed in a cast-down longing just to be done with it all. But—

*Is it really Christian hope
If I'm just a gloomy mope
On a dreary downward slope*

Who so vainly tries to grope
For a happy-Heaven rope
If it's only, just to cope?

Let's be sure the answer's "Nope!"

Consider Philippians 1:21. Paul says, *"For to me to live is Christ, and to die is gain."* *"To live is Christ"* means that his life was good—since it was about, for, with, and in, Jesus. Paul wasn't depressed; so sick of earth that he saw death as gain. Rather, he had a vibrant *"I've-got-a-great-reason-to-be-alive-on-earth-because-I-have-Christ"* faith that saw purpose in sticking around (1:22, 24-26)—even though Heaven would be far better (1:23). Paul's hope wasn't conceived in deep depression, but in joyful contentment; and in the confidence that as good as this life is, something even better awaits.

    I want that. I don't want to long for heaven just because I'm headache or sorrow-weary, but more so, because the delicious goodness of a Jesus-centered life today makes me hungry for the full meal. It's okay to mourn my pain and groan for glory (Romans 8:18-25); but if my life is Christ—being all about Him, in Him, and for Him—then I don't need to be pain-free. And if pain continues? It will remind me that while life is good now, the best is yet to be.

    Make no mistake. I do long for relief; for that World where the risen, reigning, and returning King will banish my pain, not by briefly blocking it, but by forever healing it. But I long too, and I long more, for the dear face and long embrace of the One who is getting me through. I long for the full feast of communion with the One who's nourished with His love and grace for 30 years and more. I long for enduring faith and aching hope to be lost in actual sight.

    I long that Christ will be my life today, my grace tomorrow, my Happiness forever.

Epilogue

Can I Hear a Well-Done?
(How I Live to Hear Him Say It)

*"Well done, good and faithful servant.
You have been faithful over a little; I will set you over much.
Enter into the joy of your Master."*
(Matthew 25:21)

January 11, 2019

Today's my headache-anniversary! 30 years are done. Year 31 has begun. I'll need an ellipsis, not a period.

A man once lived with us whose body was ravaged by addictions. With his waning strength he scratched out meager moments of joy amidst months of pain. "Joe" was a heavy-set battle-scarred guy who found even simple tasks hard, which explains why he asked if I'd cut his toenails. When I said "Sure!", he pulled out a pair of wire cutters. It turned out that his toenails were so thickly gnarled that no clippers would do. So there on my knees, with his feet in my hands, I wire-cut his toenails.

I remember thinking: "Jesus, without your promise of commendation, I don't think I'd be doing this. I do this gladly for Joe because I love you, *and because I hope for the Day when I'll hear you say: 'Well done Tim. You were good and faithful in all I gave you to do'"* (Matthew 25:21).

Like most, I've never been called to great exploits. I'm mostly about snipping toenails and enduring a headache with as much grace as I can; not that I would choose either. I resonate with Frodo in his trying hour, *"I wish it need not have happened in my time."* Yet, when Gandalf responds

"*So do all who live to see such times. But that is not for them to decide. All we have to decide is what to do with the time that is given us*"—I am stirred to do whatever I am asked, as well as I can. And I have been asked to do the ordinary while enduring a headache.

"So dear Father, please give grace to endure, and endure I will—if only I can hear those precious words. It is not for me to crave anything more, so long as you say, 'Tim, you cut Joe's toenails with gracious love. Well done! And Tim, about that headache: I know that it hurt and harassed you for most of your life, but you did well. You. Did. Well.'"

I wonder what God has called you to. What losses and crosses do you bear? I hope these reflections have helped to point you upward and secure your faith. I also hope they've helped to center you here: what matters is not so much what we do or experience or suffer, but that we do well whatever we're called to do, no matter the pain we feel.

And what matters still more is that we do it well, *in full conscious reliance on the present and future grace of Jesus*, which is the only way we can do well; the only way to be carried all the way home to our gracious Master's smiling face and wonderful "Well done".

So by His amazing grace, let us keep the faith and fight the fight and finish the race.

Until He comes...

Worship Worthy

Alliterative Adoration

Timothy M. Shorey

Worship Worthy: Alliterative Adoration offers Jesus-centered praise expressed through alliterative poetry. It celebrates the person and work of Jesus Christ by mixing theology with doxology to provoke adoration in the deeper levels of the heart.

This title is available at https://amzn.to/2RYvSZ7

Made in the USA
Middletown, DE
26 March 2019